THE PLATES
LE TAVOLE

GIOVANNI BATTISTA FERRARI
(1584-1655)

Malum Citreum Vulgare pl. 61 - Giovanni Baptista Ferrari

LUCA STEFANO CRISTINI

ORANGES, MANDARINS, CEDARS, LEMONS & BERGAMOTS...

FROM XVI, XVII AND XVIII CENTURIES ARTISTIC ENGRAVINGS

ARANCI, MANDARINI, CEDRI, LIMONI E BERGAMOTTI
ARTISTICI AGRUMI DALLE INCISIONI DI FERRARI, ALDROVRANDI, VOLCKHAMER..

Curious and detailed collection of images of botanical subjects belonging to the citrus family, made by artists, scientists, biologists and anthropologists. Artists of the past engaged in the realization of real museums of natural history. One of them, among the best known, the bolognese Aldrovandi called his work "theater" or "microcosm of nature," he placed at the disposal of 18.000 scholars "diversity of natural things" and 7.000 "dried plants in fifteenvolumes" . 17 volumes containing thousands of beautiful watercolors of animals, plants, minerals and monsters were part of the collection. These responded to the precise Aldrovandi and colleagues's awareness of the images' central role, as part of the research, that in their opinion were indeed very useful for the circulation of knowledge, offering a faithful portrait of the "natural things"...

DARWIN'S VIEW SERIES

Octually, the world from Darwin's point of view. The new series of Bookmoon specificallydedicated to the animal, vegetable and mineral world. A great review of nature through his most beautiful and fascinating images, taken from ancient tomes and essays about nature, made by the greatest individuals, artists and scientists together. Not only that, "Darwin's view" will involve yourself through the description of the stories, with facts and images of the exotic and romantic travels, made by the great explorers and brilliant scientists of the past, starting with the epic one on the HMS Beagle of our beloved and legendary Charles Robert Darwin!

ENGLISH & ITALIAN TEXT

DARWIN'S VIEW

BOOKMOON
ARTE-STORIA-MUSICA

ISBN: 978-88-9327-083-0   2nd edition : May 2016

Title: Bookmoon Darwin's view 001 - **Oranges, mandarins, cedars, lemons & bergamots... Artistic engravings   of Ferrari, Aldrovrandi, Volckhamer...** Serie realized by Luca S. Cristini.
Editor: Soldiershop publishing, for Bookmoon brand. Cover & Art Design: Luca S. Cristini.

ORANGES, MANDARINS, CEDARS, LEMONS & BERGAMOTS...

La Sicilia si sa, è ben rinomata per le vaste distese di agrumeti: aranci, limoni, mandarini, bergamotti, cedri ecc. In questa bellissima terra essi da sempre vengono comunemente chiamati "Giardini". Questo appellativo trovava la sua origine nella primitiva usanza che gli agrumi avevano a quei tempi e dalla natura molto ornamentale che gli aranci. Portati una prima volta in Sicilia dalla dominazione araba nel IX e XI secolo, infatti questi primi aranci erano del tipo amaro (*Citrus aurantium*), di conseguenza i frutti di queste piante non erano gradevoli al gusto. La diffusione dell'arancio dolce (*Citrus sinensis*) ebbe inizio fra la metà del 400 e il 500 a seguito dei frequenti scambi commerciali con i portoghesi. Il primo riferimento scritto sulle famose Arance Rosse risale al 1646, ed è dovuto all'opera del botanico senese Giovanni Battista Ferrari nell'opera *Hesperides,* in cui descrive per la prima volta un frutto di una varietà particolare di arance, *Aurantium Indicum*, con polpa pigmentata ("*purpurei coloris medulla*"), giunto in Sicilia grazie ad un missionario genovese di ritorno dalle Isole Filippine. I frutti citati fanno parte del nostro volume. Insieme all'opera di Ferrari, di cui parliamo più avanti è però doveroso anche citare gli altri autori delle immagini da noi pubblicate.

▲ **Vaso di limoni,** immagine tratta da *Hesperidum Norimbergensium, sive, De malorum citreorum, limonum,* ecc. insigne opera del 1713 del botanico tedesco Johann Christoph Volkamer.

Vase lemon image from Hesperidum Norimbergensium, sive, De malorum citreorum, limonum, (1713) of Johann Christoph Volkamer.

Origini e specie

Gli agrumi ed i loro frutti sono una specie botanica appartenenti alla sottofamiglia *Aurantioideae* (famiglia delle *Rutaceae*) . Ne fanno parte i seguenti generi: Citrus: arancio e arancio amaro, limone, pompelmo, mandarino, pomelo, cedro, clementina, bergamotto, chinotto, combava, limetta.
La Fortunella nelle specie: *Fortunella crassifolia, Fortunella hindsii, Fortunella japonica, Fortunella margarita, Fortunella obovata, Fortunella polyandra.* Infine il Poncirus: con un'unica specie, *Poncirus trifoliata.*

This book is mainly devoted to the historical and scientific illustration by all those fruits belonging to the citrus family. The most famous are:
Citron (Citrus medica) - This was the first Citrus fruit that was introduced to Europe by the armies of Alexander the Great about 300 BC. It found a suitable home in the Mediterranean region where it has been cultivated from that time to the present.
Grapefruit (C. paradisii) - This is a vigorous tree that reaches a height of 30 to 50 feet. It has a round, thick head of foliage. Its leaves are large, egg-shaped (ovate) and blunt pointed. Their large flowers are white and are produced singly or in axillary clusters. The fruits are larger than the Orange and are usually in bunches. They are light yellow and have silvery white or pink flesh. Grapefruit (C. paradisii) - This is a vigorous tree that reaches a height of 30 to 50 feet. It has a round, thick head of foliage. Its leaves are large, egg-shaped (ovate) and blunt pointed. Their large flowers are white and are produced singly or in axillary clusters. The fruits are larger than the Orange and are usually in bunches. They are light yellow and have silvery white or pink flesh.
Grapefruit (C. paradisii) - This is a vigorous tree that reaches a height of 30 to 50 feet. It has a round, thick head of foliage. Its leaves are large, egg-shaped (ovate) and blunt pointed. Their large flowers are white and are produced singly or in axillary clusters. The fruits are larger than the Orange and are usually in bunches. They are light yellow and have silvery white or pink flesh.
Mandarin Orange (C. nobilis deliciosa) - This small, spiny tree has thin branches and twigs. The oblate (often very flattened at the ends) fruits are orange to orange-red with a loose rind that comes off easily. The 9-15 fruit sections are loosely attached to the rind and one another. The pulp is deep orange, sweet or fairly acid.
Sour Orange (C. Aurantium) - This small, spiny tree grows up to 30 feet high and has a compact, rounded top. Its leaves are ovate and fragrant when crushed.

La sottofamiglia degli aurantioideae comprende quindi solo tre generi e diciotto specie esattamente definite e stabili (quelle qui sopra elencate), tuttavia, in natura è possibile individuare numerose varianti e mutazioni naturali, nell'infiorescenza come pure nei frutti, per cui si trovano vari tipi di agrumi in varie parti del mondo. Oltre a ciò sono stati sviluppati numerosissimi ibridi. L'origine di tutti i *Citrus* è l'India e l'Estremo Oriente, le fortunelle e il Poncirus provengono invece dalla Cina. Le varie specie hanno raggiunto l'Europa in tempi diversi. Sembra che il primo sia stato il cedro, ben noto anche tra i Romani che lo chiamavano pomo di Persia. È documentato che i Romani conoscevano già nel primo secolo pure il limone e l'arancio amaro, ma la loro coltivazione è stata introdotta nel Mediterraneo solo nel decimo secolo dai Saraceni. La coltivazione dell'arancio dolce invece è stata introdotta dai Portoghesi appena nel secolo sedicesimo, mentre risale addirittura al secolo diciannovesimo l'acquisizione del mandarino.

Giovanni Battista Ferrari (Siena 1584-1655)

*H*esperidi, sive De malorum Aureorum cultura et usa Libri Quatuor è l'opera più famosa di Giovanni Battista Ferrari. Elaborato studio dedicato agli agrumi, venne pubblicato a Roma nel 1646 ed è considerato uno dei volumi botanici più splendidi, decorativi e scientificamente precisi del XVII secolo in Europa .

Ferrari nasce a Siena nel 1583 ed è entra nella Compagnia di Gesù a Roma nel 1602. Viene nominato consigliere *Horticultural* presso la famiglia papale, e gli si affida la gestione del nuovo giardino di Palazzo Barberini a Roma. In questo famoso giardino sono presenti rare w nuovissime piante appena scoperte nel nuovo mondo, in Africa e in Asia. Questo trattato sugli agrumi include le più svariate e curiose varietà di piante, ordinate in precise ed elaborate coltivazioni. *Hesperidi* rifletté quindi il crescente interesse che nel Seicento ruotava attorno alle serre di aranceti. Questa coltivazione, attenta alla delicatezza di questi alberi, teneva ovviamente conto dei climi freddi del nord Europa e quelli assai più favorevoli delle estati italiane.

Ferrari è anche noto per il trattato *Flora, seu De florum cultura lib. 4*, pubblicato dapprima in lingua latina nel

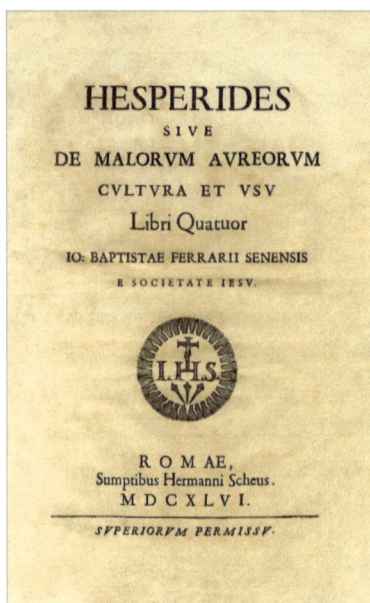

HESPERIDES
SIVE
DE MALORVM AVREORVM
CVLTVRA ET VSV
Libri Quatuor
IO: BAPTISTAE FERRARII SENENSIS
E SOCIETATE IESV.

I.H.S.

ROMAE,
Sumptibus Hermanni Scheus.
MDCXLVI.
SVPERIORVM PERMISSV.

▲ **Frontespizio** del famoso libro *Hesperides*, che insieme a *Flora, seu De florum cultura* rappresentano i volumi più interessanti eseguito dallo scienziato senese Giovanni Battista Ferrari.
Frontispiece of the famous book Hesperides, with Flora, seu De Florum culture are the most interesting volumes carried by the Tuscanian scientist .

The fruit is orange or reddish-orange with a rind that is rough, strong scented and bitter.

Sour Orange (C. Aurantium) - This small, spiny tree grows up to 30 feet high and has a compact, rounded top. Its leaves are ovate and fragrant when crushed. The fruit is orange or reddish-orange with a rind that is rough, strong scented and bitter.

Origins and species

*C*itrus is a common term and genus (Citrus) of flowering plants in the rue family, Rutaceae. Citrus is believed to have originated principally in India and China. the best-known examples are the oranges, lemons, grapefruit, and limes. The generic name originated in Latin, where it specifically referred to the plant now known as Citron (C. medica). It was derived from the ancient Greek word for cedar,(kédros). Collectively, Citrus fruits and plants are also known by the Romance loanword agrumes (literally "sour fruits").

The taxonomy and systematics of the genus are complex and the precise number of natural species is unclear, as many of the named species are hybrids clonally propagated through seeds (by apomixis), and there is genetic evidence that even some wild, true-breeding species are of hybrid origin. Natural and cultivated origin hybrids include commercially important fruit such as the oranges, grapefruit, lemons, some limes, and some tangerines. Research suggests that the closely related genus Fortunella (kumquats), and perhaps also Poncirus and the Australian Microcitrus and Eremocitrus, should be included in Citrus; most botanists now classify Microcitrus and Eremocitrus as part of the genus Citrus.

Giovanni Battista Ferrari (Siena 1584-1655)

*H*esperides, sive, De Malorum Aureorum cultura et usa Libri Quatuor are a work of Giovanni Battista Ferrari's This work of citrus was published in Rome in 1646 and is regarded as one of the most splendid, scientifically precise and decorative botanical works of seventeenth-century Europe.

Ferrari was born in Sienna in 1584, was an Italian Jesuit and professor in Rome, a botanist, and an author of illustrated botanical books and a Latin-

1633 e ristampato in traduzione italiana nel 1638 col titolo *Flora ouero Cultura di fiori del p. Gio. Battista Ferrari sanese della Comp. di Giesù distinta in quattro libri e trasportata dalla lingua latina nell'italiana* da Lodovico Aureli Perugino. Molta importanza dei lavori del Ferrari sono dovuti anche alla caratura dei collaboratori che presero parte alla loro realizzazione. Le brillantissime tavole di questi sacri testi della botanica appartengono infatti ad alcuni fra i più importanti artisti dell'epoca: Cornelius Bolemaert, Pietro da Cortona, Andrea Sacchi, Nicolas Poussin, Guido Reni e altri. Il tema principale di quest'opera rimane la audace comparazione fra il giardino delle Esperidi e la nascita dell'eta dell'oro del giardino italiano, magnificamente rappresentato in primis da quello della famiglia Barberini.

Ulisse Aldrovandi (Bologna 1522-1605)

Colonna della scienza e della naturalistica barocca, ma non solo, Ulisse Aldrovandi, talvolta scritto Aldovrandi, è stato un naturalista, botanico ed entomologo italiano, realizzatore di uno dei primi musei di storia naturale, studioso delle diversità del mondo vivente, esploratore che, negli ultimi decenni del Cinquecento e fino ai primi del Seicento, si impose come una delle maggiori figure della scienza, nonché guida e riferimento per i naturalisti italiani contemporanei.

A lui fra le altre cose si deve il conio del termine geologia, avvenuto nel 1603 ! Nato da una nobile famiglia bolognese, Ulisse manifestò una spiccata personalità fin da bambino: a soli 12 anni, "senza saputa de' suoi, si partì senza denari, con animo ardito et giunse a Roma"…

Tornato a Bologna nel 1539, dopo aver compiuto un'epico viaggio fino a Santiago de Compostella, s'iscrisse all'Università per studiarvi Lettere con i nomi più dotti del tempo. Ma è solo nel 1549, che sempre a Bologna egli fa la conoscenza del botanico imolese Luca Ghini, che lo iniziò all'interesse per le piante. Accusato di eresia con altri concittadini - non è noto con quali precise imputazioni - fu arrestato il 12 giugno e costretto all'abiura in San Petronio il 1° settembre; ciò nonostante, insieme con altri due imputati, fu condotto a Roma per subire un nuovo processo ma, morto in

▲ **Ritratto di Ulisse Aldrovandi,** illustre scienziato bolognese che si occupò dello scibile umano in ogni sua forma, spesso anche di interessi distanti fra loro, tanta era la sua innata curiosità.

Portrait of Ulisse Aldrovandi, a renowned scientist from Bologna who took care of human knowledge in all its forms, often of interest away from each other, such was his innate curiosity.

Syrian dictionary. In 1602. as Horticultural Advisor to the Papal family he was appointed to manage the newly formed garden at the Barberini Palace in Rome. The famed Barberini garden displayed the newly found plants from the most recent voyages of trade and discovery. Rare plants from America, Asia, and Africa were all cultivated, showcased and named at this important Roman garden. This treatise on citrus included many varieties of rare plants and recorded the elaborately detailed planting, training and housing methods. Hesperides reflected the growing interest in seventeenth-century orangeries, forerunner of the greenhouse. The orangeries were needed to keep delicate trees alive during the cold Northern European winters and the hot Italian summers.

Hesperides Sive de MalorumAureorum Cultura is considered Ferrari's second greatest achievement. It was a collaboration with one of Rome's leading scholars and various patrons dedicated to the establishment of extensive precise taxonomic data relating to citrus. Hesperides includes eighty brilliantly engraved botanical citrus plates, composed round and in section, by the foremost artist and engravers of the period: Cornelius Bolemaert, Pietro da Cortona, Andrea Sacchi, Nicolas Poussin, and Guido Reni all contributed to this masterpiece of science and art.

The main theme of this work was the comparison of the mythical garden of the Hesperides with the development of the "Golden Age" of the Italian garden which coincided with the reign of the Barberini family.

Ulisse Adrovandi (Bologna 1522-1605)

*U*lisse Aldrovandi (1522 – 1605) was an Italian naturalist, the ideator and creator of the Bologna's botanical garden, one of the first in Europe. Carolus Linnaeus and the comte de Buffon reckoned him the father of natural history studies. He is usually referred to, especially in older literature, as Aldrovandus; his name in Italian is equally given as Aldroandi or Aldovrandi. In the course of his life he would assemble one of the most spectacular cabinets of curiosities, his "theatre" illuminating natural history comprising some 7000 specimens of the *diversità di cose naturali*, of which he

quel frangente Paolo III e succedutogli Giulio III, l'Aldovrandi fu fortunosamente prosciolto…A Roma la sua anima inquieta lo portò ad interessarsi di statue antiche, pesci, piante e ..mostri. Tra il 1551 ed il 1554, la botanica ebbe tuttavia la meglio ed egli organizzò numerose spedizioni di raccolta di piante: questa collezione è oggi nota come Erbario di Ulisse Aldrovandi. Acquistata giusta fama Ad Aldrovandi riuscì quanto non era riuscito a Luca Ghini, medico ed eminente botanico cinquecentesco suo iniziatore all'amore per le piante. Su sua proposta il Senato bolognese istituì nel 1568 l'Orto Pubblico, che fu diretto per i suoi primi 38 anni dall'Aldrovandi stesso. La prima sede dell'Orto fu nel centro della città, all'interno del Palazzo Pubblico, in un cortile che si trovava vicino all'aula dove Aldrovandi impartiva le sue lezioni. Il preciso e attento lavoro di raccolta e conservazione di reperti naturalistici portò alla realizzazione di uno dei primi musei di storia naturale, definito dall'Aldrovandi stesso "teatro", o "microcosmo di natura", in cui si potevano studiare ed osservare ben 18.000 "diversità di cose naturali" e oltre 7.000 "piante essiccate in quindici volumi". Alcuni degli splendidi acquerelli raffiguranti gli agrumi presentati in questo volume appartengono proprio a questo enorme classificatore. Dopo la sua morte, avvenuta nel 1605, gli fu dedicata una specie botanica: L'Aldrovanda vesiculosa, una specie di pianta carnivora acquatica.

Volckamer, Muntig, Redouté e Weinmann

La Nostra selezione di stampe comprende anche lavori di altri illustri botanici. A cominciare dal tedesco Johann Cristoph Volckamer (1644-1720) autore del già citato *Hesperidum Norimbergensium, sive, De malorum citreorum, limonum*.
Per proseguire poi con Abraham Munting (1626 - 1683) medico e botanico olandese, autore di numerosi testi dedicati a fiori, frutti e piante.
Ed ancora, Johann Wilhelm Weinmann (1683 - 1741), farmacista e botanico tedesco, cui si deve la nota opera: *florilegium Phytanthoza iconographia* illustratissimo lavoro con centinaia di aquerelli botanici di pregevole fattura.
Per finire con le opere dell'artista e botanico francese Pierre Joseph Redoutè (1759-1840).

▲ Bella illustrazione di agrumi, opera di Pierre-Joseph Redouté (1759 – 1840) illustre pittore e botanico francese.

Beautiful illustration of citrus, by Pierre-Joseph Redouté (1759 - 1840) famous French painter and botanist.

wrote a description in 1595. Between 1551 and 1554 he organised several expeditions to collect plants for a herbarium, among the first botanizing expeditions. Eventually his herbarium contained about 4760 dried specimens on 4117 sheets in sixteen volumes, preserved at the University of Bologna. He also had various artists, including Jacopo Ligozzi, Giovanni Neri, and Cornelio Schwindt, make illustrations of specimens.
At his demand and under his direction a public botanic garden was created in Bologna in 1568, now the Orto Botanico dell'Università di Bologna. Due to a dispute on the composition of a popular medicine with the pharmacists and doctors of Bologna in 1575 he was suspended from all public position for five years. In 1577 he sought the aid of pope Gregory XIII (a cousin of his mother) who wrote to the authorities of Bologna to reinstate Aldrovandi in his public offices and request financial aid to help him publish his books.

Volckamer, Muntig, Redouté e Weinmann

Johann Christoph Volkamer (June 7, 1644 – August 26, 1720) was a German merchant, manufacturer and botanist.He published 1708-1714 a very famous two volume work over citrus under the title "Nurenbergische Hesperides, the thorough description of the noble Citron, used in within and neighbouring area, praised Lemon, and Orange fruits, like such, be received and carried away, velvet of a detailed dicription of most sorts, which some were brought to Nuremberg actually grown, others by different strange places there... "
Johann Wilhelm Weinmann (1683 - 1741), apothecary and botanist, is noted for his creation of the florilegium Phytanthoza iconographia between 1737 and 1745, an ambitious project which resulted in eight folio volumes with more than 1 000 hand-coloured engravings of several thousand plants.
Abraham Munting (1626-1683) was a physician, botanist, Professor Dutch. Academically worked in Groningen. And last, some images are from the finest work of Pierre-Joseph Redouté (1759 – 1840), was a Belgian painter and botanist, known for his watercolours of roses, lilies and other flowers at Malmaison. He was nicknamed "The Raphael of flowers".

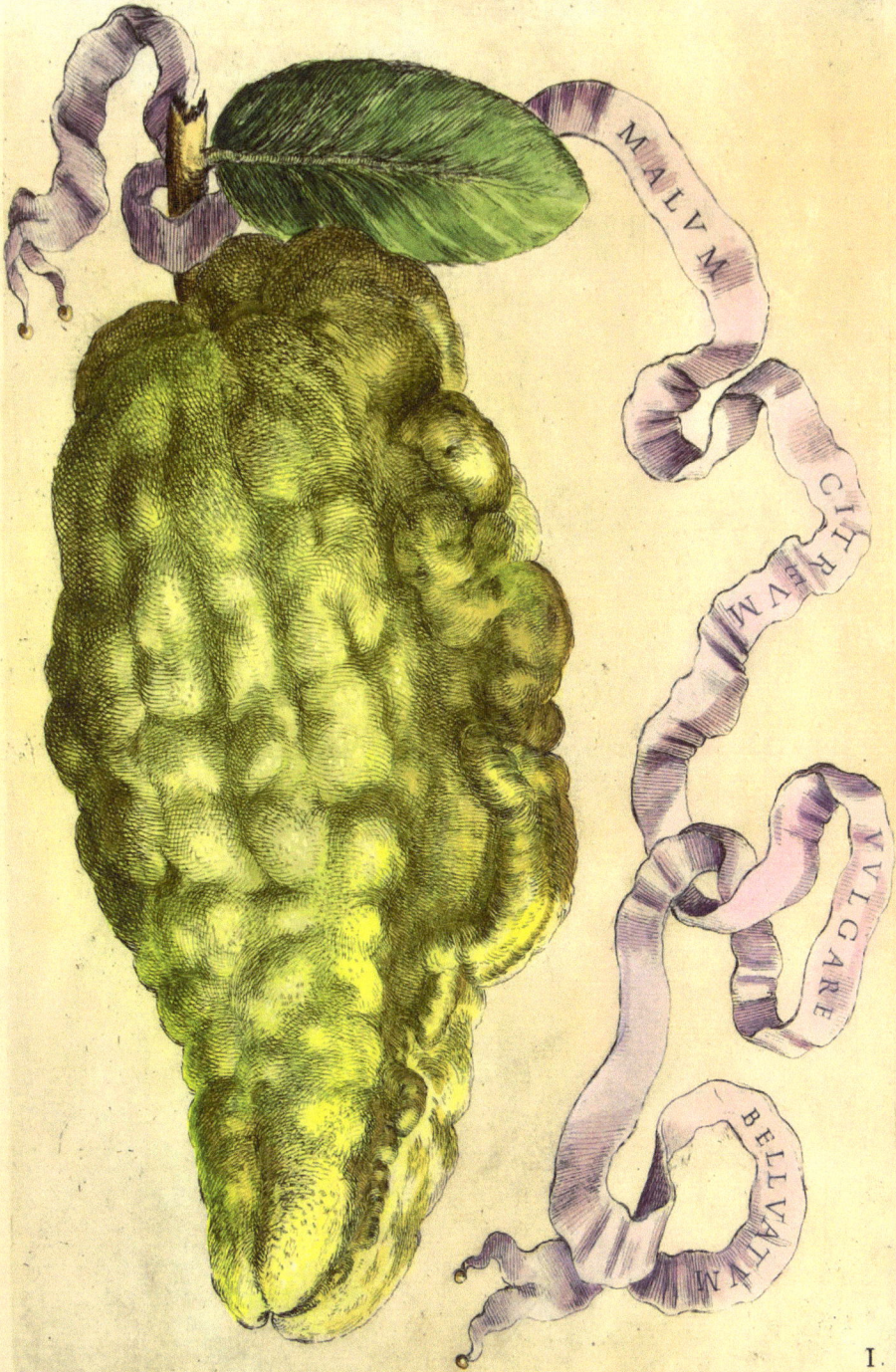

MALVM CITREVM VVLGARE BELLVATVM

I.

Malum Citreum Vulgare Bellatum pl. 65 - Giovanni Baptista Ferrari

Aurantium Corniculatum pl. 409 - Giovanni Baptista Ferrari

73

MALVM

CITREVM

DVLCI

MEDVLLA

K.

Malum Citreum Dulci Medulla pl. 73 - Giovanni Baptista Ferrari

LIMONIAE FLORES

Limoniae Flores pl. 189 - Giovanni Baptista Ferrari

LIMON VVLGARIS

Limon Vulgaris pl. 193 - Giovanni Baptista Ferrari

197

LIMON

S. REMI

Limon S.Remi pl. 197 - Giovanni Baptista Ferrari

LIMON LIGVRIAE CERIESCVS

Limon Liguriae Ceriescus pl. 199 - Giovanni Baptista Ferrari

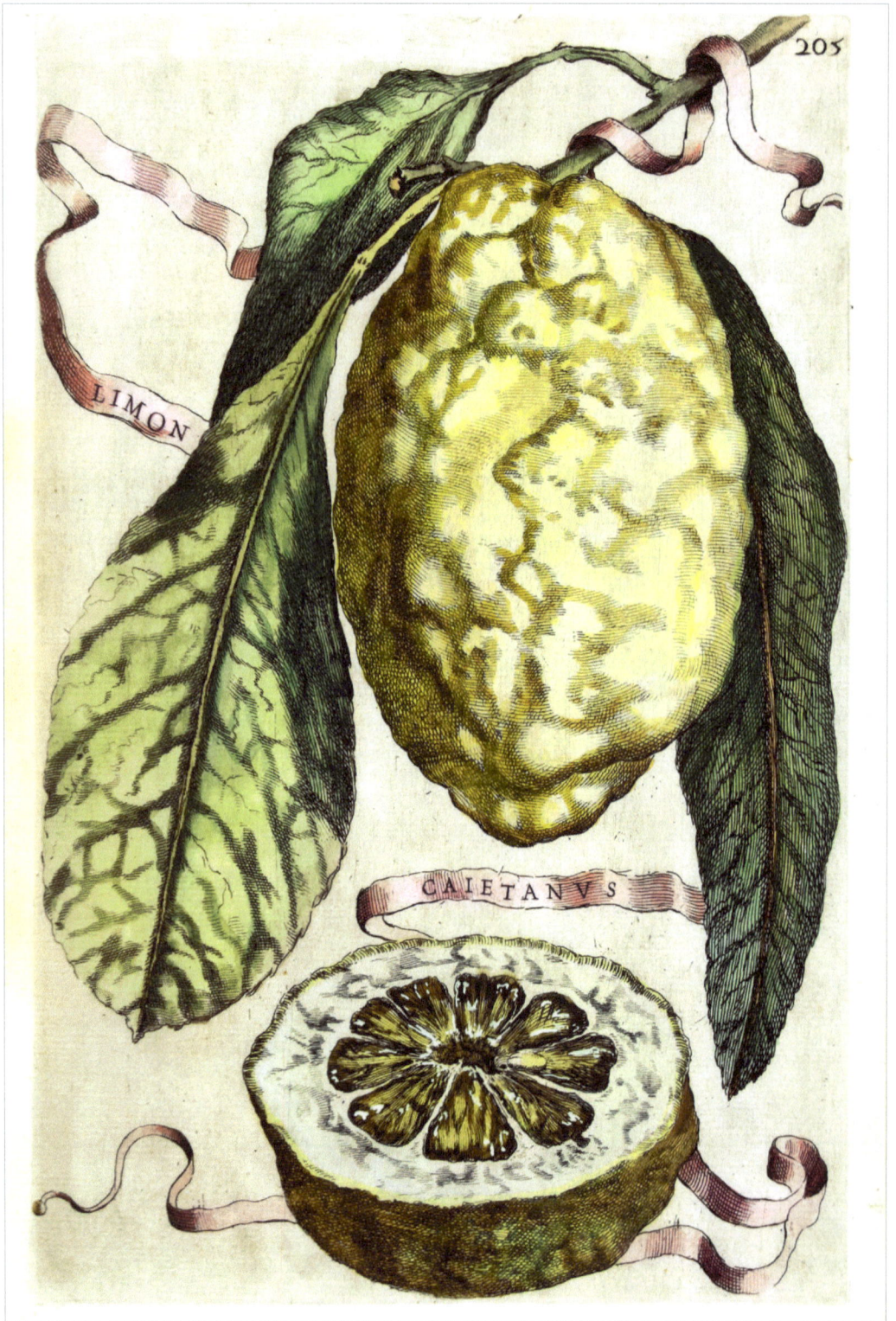

205

LIMON

CAIETANVS

Limon Caietanus pl. 205 - Giovanni Baptista Ferrari

LIMON

AMALPHITANVS

Limon Amalphitanus pl. 207 - Giovanni Baptista Ferrari

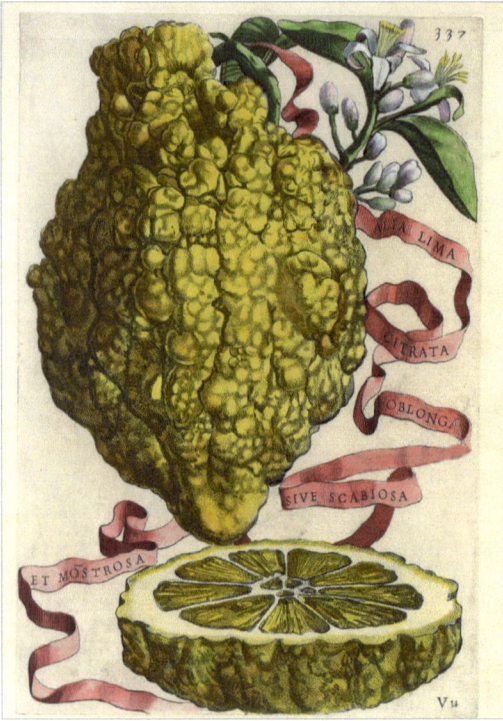

219

LIMON LAVRAE

Ee 2

Limon Lauraes pl. 219 - Giovanni Baptista Ferrari

LIMON

PERIALIS

Ff

Limon Imperialis pl. 225 - Giovanni Baptista Ferrari

LIMON

DVLCI MEDVLLA

VVLGARIS

Limon Dulci Medualla Vulgariss pl. 229 - Giovanni Baptista Ferrari

237

LIMON

PERETTAE CONSIMILIS

Limon Perettae Consimilis pl. 237 - Giovanni Baptista Ferrari

LIMON
RACEMOSVS

Hh 2

Limon Racemosus pl. 243 - Giovanni Baptista Ferrari

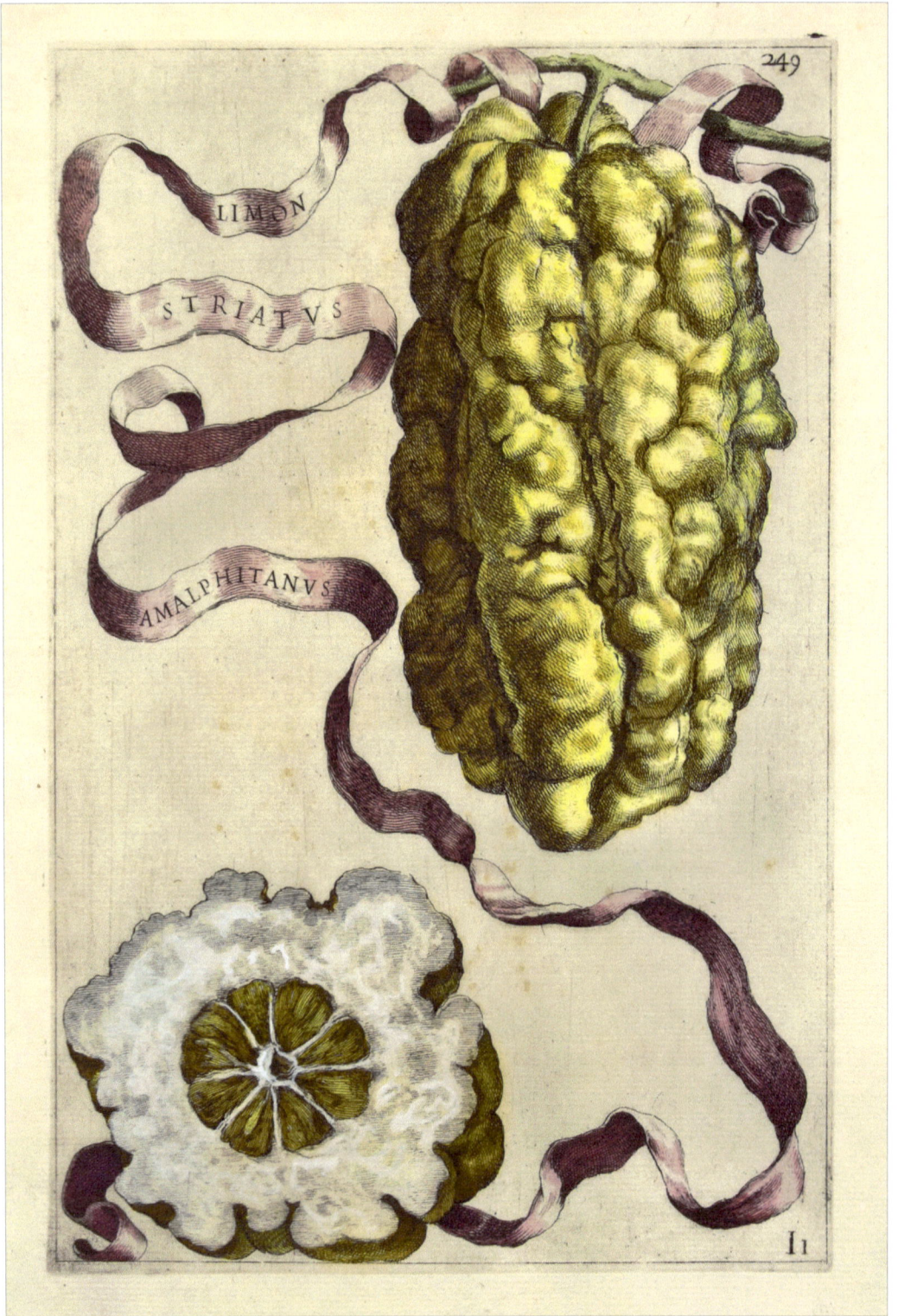

LIMON

STRIATVS

AMALPHITANVS

249

I1

Limon Striatus Amalphitanuss pl. 249 - Giovanni Baptista Ferrari

Limon Sbardonius pl. 253 - Giovanni Baptista Ferrari

LIMON

ROSOLINVS

Limon Rosolinuss pl. 255 - Giovanni Baptista Ferrari

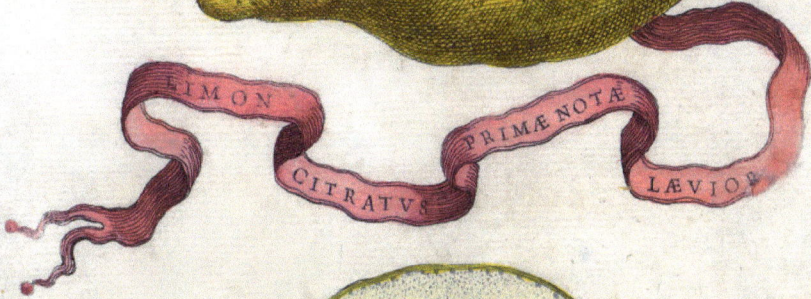

LIMON CITRATVS PRIMÆ NOTÆ LÆVIOR

LL

Limon Citratus Primae Notae Lavior pl. 265 - Giovanni Baptista Ferrari

269

LIMON CITRATVS ALTERVM INCLVDENS

Limon Citratus Alterum Includens pl. 265 - Giovanni Baptista Ferrari

LIMON CITRATVS

AMALPHITANVS

Nn

Limon Citratus Amalphitanus pl. 281 - Giovanni Baptista Ferrari

TYBERIM

TRANS

IN COENOBIO

LIMON CITRATVS

TERESIANO

N n 2

Limon Citratus in Coenobio Teresiano pl. 283 - Giovanni Baptista Ferrari

Limon Pseudocitratus Barberinorum pl. 285 - Giovanni Baptista Ferrari

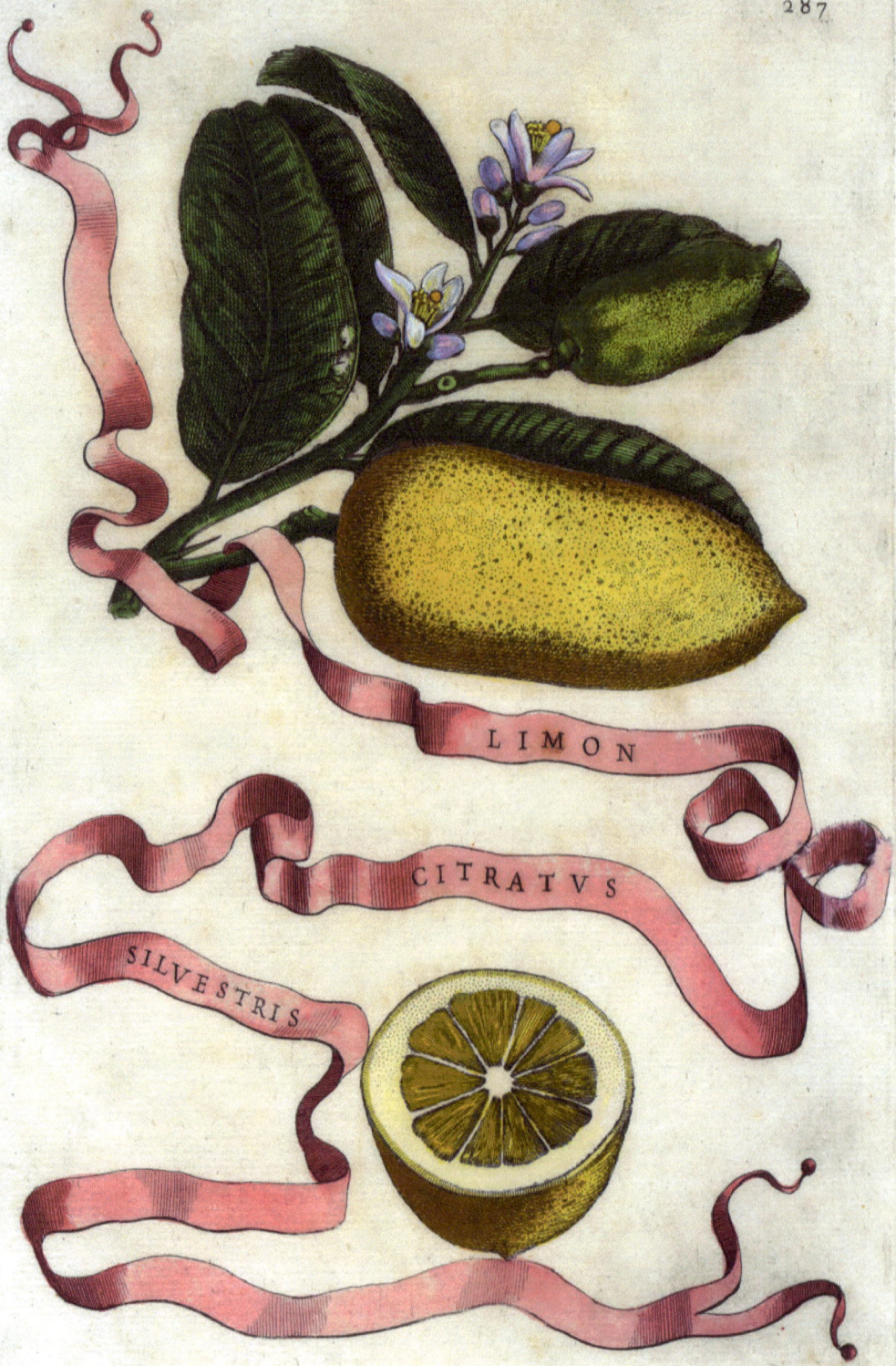

LIMON

CITRATVS

SILVESTRIS

Limon Citratus Silvestris pl. 287 - Giovanni Baptista Ferrari

LIMON

PONZINVS

LIGVSTICVS

Oo 2

Limon Ponzinus Ligusticus pl. 291 - Giovanni Baptista Ferrari

LIMON PONZINVS

RVBENS

Limon Ponzinus Rubens pl. 293 - Giovanni Baptista Ferrari

LIMON

PONZINV

CHALCEDONIVS

P p

Limon Ponzinus Chalcedonius pl. 297 - Giovanni Baptista Ferrari

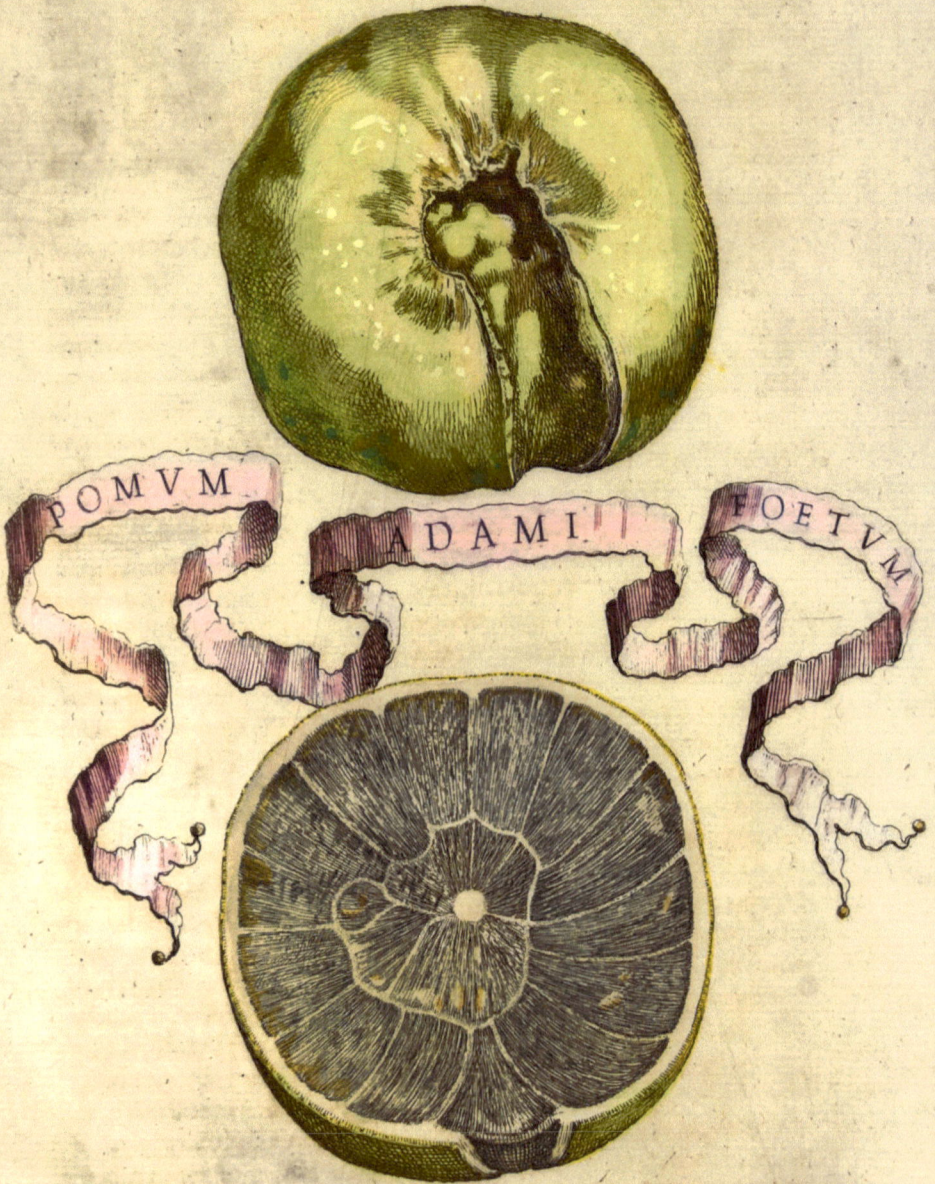

POMVM ADAMI FOETVM

Pomum Adami Foetum pl. 315 - Giovanni Baptista Ferrari

LVMIA
VALENTINA

SS

Lumia Valentina pl. 321 - Giovanni Baptista Ferrari

Lumia Salis Sive Spatafora pl. 325 - Giovanni Baptista Ferrari

LVMIA OLLVLAE ASPECTV

Lumia Ollulae Aspectu pl. 327 - Giovanni Baptista Ferrari

MEDVLLAE

EXPERS

LVMIA

Tt

Lumia Expers Medullae pl. 329 - Giovanni Baptista Ferrari

Lima Romana Piorum in Hortis pl. 335 - Giovanni Baptista Ferrari

BBb

Arantium Acri Dulcique Medulla Vulgare pl. 377 - Giovanni Baptista Ferrari

FLORE

AVRANTIVM

DVPLICI

Aurantium Flore Duplici pl. 391 - Giovanni Baptista Ferrari

383

339

LIMA EADEM ROTVNDA

389

479

Citrus Various - Giovanni Baptista Ferrari

AVRANTIVM FOETIFERVM

Aurantium Foetiferum pl. 405 - Giovanni Baptista Ferrari

423

AVRANTIVM CITRATVM

Aurantium Citratum pl. 423 - Giovanni Baptista Ferrari

THE PLATES
LE TAVOLE

ULISSE ALDROVANDI (1522-1605)
ABRAHAM MUNTING (1626 - 1683)
JOHANN CRISTOPH VOLCKAMER (1644-1720)
JOHANN WILHELM WEINMANN (1683 - 1741)
PIERRE JOSEPH REDOUTÈ (1759-1840)

C itrium oblongum n.°.1.
C itrium rotundum.n.°.2.

Citrium Oblungum et Rorundum - Ulisse Aldrovandi

Citrium pyriforme longitudine dodrantis circumferentia duorum dodrantum pondere quinq librarū

Citrium Pyriforme Longitude - Ulisse Aldrovandi

Fig. 2.

Orange - Abraham Munting

Malus Citria Cornuta - Abraham Munting

1. Das Waßer-Rad. 2. Platz der fünf Columnen milliarien. 3. Das Pomerantzen-Hauß. 4. Die Sonnen-Uhr von Buxs. 5. Der Irrgarten. 6. Das Schild Crotten Weyerlein. 7. Obeliscus Constantinopolitinus auß einem stuck stein 20 k schuhlang.

Giardini e serre di agrumi da *Nurenbergische Hesperides* - 1713 - Johann Christoph Volkamer.

Eufferlicher Profpect
des Obfervatory auf der
Veften

Eufferlicher Profpect VKH 103 - Johann Criftoph Volckamer

Cedro grosso Bondolotto.

NÜRNBERG.

Cedro Grosso Bondolotto VKH 114 - Johann Cristoph Volckamer

Cedro a Dittela

Cedro a Dittela VKH 116 - Johann Cristoph Volckamer

Cedro grande Lissi Bondolotto

1. Gibezenhoff. 2. Sandreuth. 3. Da brante der Wald.

Cedro Grande Lissi Bondolotto VKH 120 - Johann Cristoph Volckamer

La parte interiore del medemo Cedro

Der Schießplaz zu Werth und der Kirch hoff.

Parte interiore del medesimo cedro VKH 120 - Johann Cristoph Volckamer

Pal.zo nella Paroch: de Fiesso del Illust: S. Tornieri.

I. C. Dehne. fe.

Limon Ponzino da Valenza VKH 126 - Johann Cristoph Volckamer

Limon Zattelle

Limon Zattelle VKH 146 - Johann Cristoph Volckamer

Aranzo Gran Sorte VKH 184 - Johann Cristoph Volckamer

Aranzo Agostarolo . 1696 .

Das Hallerschlößlein.

Aranzo Agostarolo VKH 184 - Johann Cristoph Volckamer

Pomo da Sina

pag. 194. C.

Dirn Schmids Garten.

Pomo da Sina VKH 194 - Johann Cristoph Volckamer

Aranzo Limonato.

Des Herren von Lempen Hauss-Garten.

I. C. Steinberger fecit.

Aranzo Limonato VKH 202 - Johann Cristoph Volckamer

pag. 202. C.

Aranzo di Fior e Scorza doppia.

Der Geyßliſche Garten bey Wehrt.

Aranzo di Fior e Scorza doppia VKH 202 - Johann Cristoph Volckamer

Aranzo Distorto o Mostruoso VKH 206 - Johann Cristoph Volckamer

a. Malus Armeniaca, Abricotier, Marillen.
b. Malus Armeniaca fructu majore nucleo dulci, Abricotier, Abri-
cosenbaum. c. Malus Armeniaca fructu minore
d. Malus Armeniaca fructu ex luteo rubescente, Abricose, Marillen.
e. Malus Aurantia cortice dulci cauli.
f. Malus Aurantia limonis effigie.

Malus Armeniaca WN698 - Johann Weinmann

a..*Malus Aurantia citrata*, Pompelmoss .
b.*Malus Aurantia striis aureis distincta* .
c.*Malus Aurantia citrata, variegata seu mixta* .

Malus Aurantia Citrata WN699 - Johann Weinmann

a. *Malus Aurantia striis argenteis distincta.*
b. *Malus Aurantia Lusitanica seu Pomum Sinense, Apfel aus Sina.*
c. *Malus Aurantia folio Salicis, Pomeranze mit Weidenblättern.*
d. *Malus Aurantia monstrosa foliis et fructu variegatis, Pizarria.*
e. *Malus Aurantia Indica puniclo dicta, seu humilis.*

Malus Aurantia striis argenteis distincta WN700 - Johann Weinmann

a. Malus au = rantia hermaphrodita fructu medio citro, medioque Aurantia. b. Malus aurantia fructu me = diocri, Citron. c. Malus citria corniculata. d. Malus citria fructu magno, Citronat.

Malus aurantia hermaphrodia fructu WN701 - Johann Weinmann

a. *Malus citria cornuta fructu magno.*
b. *Malus Limonia cucumerina, Zucheta,* Cucumer, Limon.
c. *Malus Limonia fructu superficie aurantii, Pomme d'Adam,* Adams Apfel.
s.

Malus citria cornuta fructu magno WN702 - Johann Weinmann

a. Malus sive Poma Adami spinosum.
b. Malus cotonea seu Cydonia, Coigmassier schissen apfel.
c. Malus cydonia fructu cornuto, Coignier, gehörnte schitten.

Malus sive Poma Adami Spinosum WN703 - Johann Weinmann

Fig. 1.

A

Fig. 2.

B.

CITRUS.   CITRONIER.

Citrus Citronier T.7 nr. 31 - Pierre Joseph Redouté

CITRUS Bigaradia bizarro.   **CITRONIER** Bigaradier bizarre.

Citrus Bigaradia Bizarro T.7 nr. 36 - Pierre Joseph Redouté

CITRUS Medica   CITRONIER de Médie

Citrus Medica T.7 nr. 22 - Pierre Joseph Redouté

Fig 1.

Fig 2.

Fig 3.

Fig. 4.

Fig 6.

Fig 5.

CITRUS.   CITRONIER.

Citrus T.7 nr. 30 - Pierre Joseph Redouté

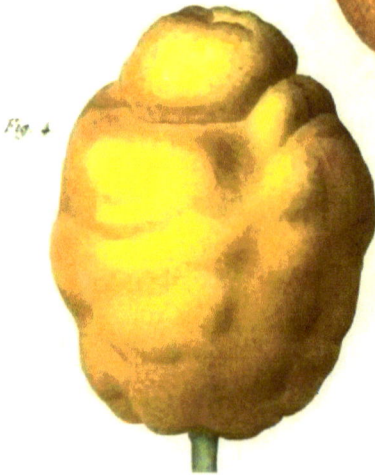

CITRUS.   CITRONIER.

Citrus Citronier T.7 nr. 24 - Pierre Joseph Redouté

CITRUS Decumana.   CITRONIER Pompelmous

Citrus Decumana T.7 nr. 42 - Pierre Joseph Redouté

CITRUS Bigaradia Sinensis   **CITRONIER** Bigaradier Chinois

Citrus Bigardia Sinesis T. 7 nr. 25 - Pierre Joseph Redouté

T. 7. N° 27
CITRUS Limonum — CITRONIER Limonier

T. 7. N° 28
CITRUS Limonum — CITRONIER Limonier

T. 7. N° 32
CITRUS Bigarradia — CITRONIER Bigarrade

T. 7. N° 38
CITRUS decumana — CITRONIER Pompelmous

Citrus Various - Pierre Joseph Redouté

TITOLI PUBBLICATI - ALREADY PUBLISHING

Della stessa collana

Fiori, farfalle, insetti, bruchi e serpenti ... Dalle superbe incisioni di Sybilla Merian e Moses Hariss

In quegli anni, l'Europa brulicava di roghi impegnati a far piazza pulita di streghe. Nel contempo una giovane scienziata: Sybilla Merian, figlia del notissimo incisore tedesco Mattheus Merian, era invece impegnata a studiare, e magnificamente illustrare il microscopico mondo di insetti, bruchi e farfalle e quello un pò più grande di fiori, vegetali e animali. La meravigliosa metamofosi dei bruchi fu alla base del suo lavoro più riuscito:
Metamorphosis insectorum Surinamensium, pubblicato ad Amsterdam nel 1705. Il lavoro realizzato da Sibylla Merian è fantastico. In effetti, in quel tempo, era inusuale occuparsi d'insetti – le bestie di Satana. I suoi disegni di piante, serpenti, ragni, iguane e coleotteri tropicali sono tuttora considerati dei capolavori e vengono ricercati dai collezionisti di tutto il mondo. Completano il volume anche interessanti incisioni di una altro grande maestro, l'entomologo inglese Moses Hariss.